WRITING LETTERS for the BLIND

WRITING LETTERS for the BLIND

Gary Fincke

Winner of the 2003 The Ohio State University Press
The Journal Award in Poetry

The Ohio State University Press • COLUMBUS

Library of Congress Cataloging-in-Publication Data

Fincke, Gary.
Writing letters for the blind / Gary Fincke.
p. cm.
ISBN 0-8142-0950-5 (hardcover : alk. paper)
I. Title.
PS3556.I457 W75 2003
811'.54—dc21

2003005785

Paper (ISBN: 978-0-8142-5120-1)
Cover by Janna Thompson Chordas
Type set in Granjon

CONTENTS

6

ACKNOWLEDGMENTS

"Dragging the Forest"	*North American Review*
"The Beatitudes of Sight"	*Poetry Northwest*
"The Fathers I Could See from My Room"	*Witness*
"What Color Did"	*Poetry*
"The Twenty-Four Hour Day" (sequence)	*Denver Quarterly*
"Playing Sleepless"	*Poet Lore*
"The Billion Heartbeats of the Mammal"	*American Scholar*
"Marking the Body"	*The Southern Review*
"The Vanishing of Forlorn Hope"	*Smartish Pace*
"The Extension of the Dead"	*Poetry*
"The Resurrection Manual"	*The Southern Review*
"The Busy Darkness" (sequence)	*The Cresset*
"Writing Letters for the Blind"	*American Scholar*
"The Era of the Vari-Vue"	*Oxford Magazine* (Pushcart Prize)
"Pushing the Black Thread"	*The Southern Review*
"Running Through Directions"	*Witness*
"The Plagues in Order"	*Smartish Pace*
"Never Again" (sequence)	*The Southern Review*
"The Brain Shelter"	*Poetry Northwest*
"Distraction Therapy"	*Prairie Schooner*
"The Piecework of Writing" (sequence)	*The Literary Review*
"The Early History of the Submarine"	*The Paris Review*
"Otherwise Healthy"	*Mid-American Review*
"How's It Going?"	*Two Rivers Review*
"The Magpie Evening"	*Prairie Schooner*

1

Dragging the Forest

After the First Aid Meet, after our patrol
Revived Mike Hofaker, who played the victim,
My father, the Scoutmaster, settled us down
With our scores for bringing back the heart and lungs.
Correctly, we'd stopped bleeding, and perfectly,
We'd treated shock. We'd made splints from newspapers
And neckerchiefs, eased them around our problem's
Broken bones and carried Mike Hofaker through
The hall by makeshift stretcher to prove safety
For the judge who'd scored us second, total time.

"You think you could save someone?" my father asked,
Driving me home along the Allegheny.
I looked at the water, but my father said,
"Up there," nodding toward the steep hill of forest
Where, he started telling me, he'd spread his arms
And walked in a line one hundred Boy Scouts wide.
"We were flanked by men," he said, "who repeated
'Fingers touching.' The boy had been lost two days.
We hiked up, moved sideways, walked down. We sidestepped
And started up again before three boys screamed."

"The lost boy, of course, was dead," my father said.
"He was tied naked to a tree, eleven
Copies of the out-of-date *Sun Telegraphs*
Folded up inside his bag like an address."
I thought my father meant me to be careful.
From where we were driving the river was black,
The woods thin enough to take the sun's last light.
Scores came on the radio. The teams were Pitt,
Army, Syracuse, Notre Dame. From bottom
To top, the width of the woods went to shadow.

The Beatitudes of Sight

With a minute to memorize, standing
    closer than the line
taped to the cement floor, I repeated
    D B O E V
and F G T E D M to myself,
    ready for the patch
to each eye, reciting for the school nurse
    who said, every time,
"Start with the smallest letters you can see."

My father taught me the beatitudes
    of sight, how the weak
who wore glasses inherited contempt.
    I learned the Lord's Prayer
for better eyes, forgiveness I needed
    for the trespasses
of the lens. I said the Apostle's Creed,
    believed in keeping
weakness secret from my father who read
    signs I couldn't see
and named every invisible bird while
    my mother, who wore
thick glasses, wept about nothing I saw.

The morning the nurse said, "Start at the top
    and read what you see,"
my mouth refused the easy alphabet,
    that white-winged woman
marking her black book with the small fraction
    of my perfection,
teaching me failure, the new testament
    it gave me, wanting
to know which sins robbed sight, which deafened and
    dumbed me, preparing
to prove myself, getting ready to see.

The Fathers I Could See from My Room

The father who lifted sample cases from his car,
The father who carried a briefcase full of grief,
The father who tallied the pros and cons of spending—
What did they do in those offices where nothing
Was built, no customers to please? What changed
By their leaving early, by their sickness, retirement,
Or death? We had moved to where one father mowed
His lawn in white shirt and tie; we'd left behind
The street of fathers who entered factories
And mills at seven or three or eleven.
I knew what they did because they detailed it drunk
On weekends when the world could wait for the things
It wanted. When Sputnik circled the planet,
When the Communists made something we couldn't buy,
We watched, on the news, the melancholy arc
Of America's latest failed rocket. The fathers
Who wore suits kept doing the work that makes nothing,
And one of them, while I slept over with his son,
Brought betrayal home at midnight, what we shouldn't hear
About faithlessness. Below us, in the driveway,
His Lincoln looked like it spent all day in an office,
Like a woman had starched and ironed it. That father
Let his wife talk herself into leaving. My friend
Propped himself so long on his elbows I wanted
Something like mumbles to squeeze under the door,
Sounds so simple they could turn into regret.

What Color Did

When disease strikes, it is because the colors of the body's elements have fallen out of balance.
—Dinshash Ghadiali, inventor of the Spectro-Chrome

Color mattered. My father held out shirts
And ties like a ring-bearer and waited
For my mother to match. And while she was
Deciding, he offered her socks and pants,
The two sport coats he owned in brown and blue.
In the early days of the pastel shirt
For men, my father seemed too old for choice,
The simple era of the white shirt gone,
This time for good, so much depending on
Color, it was almost medicinal,
Curing shyness, uncertainty and fear.

Not the first time for that. *Normalating,*
As Dinshash put it, was what color did—
In other words, therapy for the sick.
See, he advertised, the elements most
Common in us are linked to hues: The red
Of hydrogen, the blue of oxygen,
Carbon's stoplight yellow, nitrogen's green.
See, he explained, shining filtered light bulbs
On the skin above his patient's organs,
Here is the way to brighten or dim them,
Regulating the rainbow in ourselves.

Color mattered. My father faltered when
Patterns came to his shirts, pinstripes and plaids,
Madras and paisley and fields of flowers
That made a perfect match impossible.
Close enough, my mother would say, holding
Those shirts and ties to the natural light.
Close enough, yet my father turned tight-lipped
In public from her doubt, unbalanced through
Sundays until he pulled on the full green

Of his uniform for work, sweeping up
After children who wore clothes like models.

Not the first time for that. Dependable—
What the boss called him as he aligned desks,
Arranged chalk by color while my mother,
At last, purchased "The Healing Scarf," praising
Its silk and its rainbows dyed to contain
Every shade needed for recovery.
She studied its guide to color's power.
She learned the locations for pain. She wore
The scarf on her skull to balance her brain's
Intricate rainbow, and trusted the shade
Of X rays, the felt color of chemo.

Then my mother died, her rainbow of clothes
Packed and donated. My father recalled
Three combinations, washing and ironing
The plain shirts—blue, beige, and gray—laying them
Out with the ties and socks on my sister's
Unused bed, repeating them fourteen times
Through a year of Sundays and twice during
The six Wednesdays of Lent, rotating through
Good Friday and Christmas and Thanksgiving,
Funerals and weddings, as many as
Twenty times a year then, the simple shades
What he knew of color, dressing himself
Three ways for God, one for work, until he
Became all silence, unbalanced, and dark.

The Twenty-Four Hour Day

THE HISTORY OF SLEEP DEPRIVATION

1

Kept awake, all of the puppies died by
Day six. Hypothermia. Disorders
Of the brain. Sicknesses encouraged by
Fatigue and science. Which saved the next dogs.

Which earned them, after their days of testing,
Permission to drop and nap, every one
Of them recuperating except those,
The tester wrote, "that never awakened."

2

To stay awake, like dogs, you keep moving.
Do something with yourself. Keep busy. Work.
After a few days, you'll kick the habit
Of the private pornography of sleep.

Among tested humans, there's no record
Of death. Not under controlled conditions.
Not while a scientist was standing by
To list the likely uses of less sleep.

3

Once, I watched my wife carry our daughter
Through the dark house as if the next footstep
Might be the one to quiet her. We drove
For miles because her brother, at that age,

Had fallen asleep within blocks. Even
At three, he slept in his safety seat while
She screamed herself to wheezing's hospital.

And now our dog, at fourteen, sleeps more than
Twenty hours a day. I've counted, awake
All night with asthma and anxiety.
From outside comes the yard-by-yard alarm
Of barking. Like the human telegraphs

Who shouted the news of armies from farm
To farm, those dogs deliver the details
Of research through our neighborhood. Close your eyes,
They growl, then howl their lullaby: Sleep. Sleep.

LABOR OF LOVE

In my family's stories,
Labor of love is working
Two shifts and sleeping the third,
The two jobs separated
By half hours of fast walking,
Storms or snow drifts critical
To those fables because home
Was miles from every work site:
The mill, the rail yard, the shop.

After sixteen hours, after
The walking, five hours of sleep
And the leftover minutes
For the whatnot of each dawn,
Saturday was that moment
When the hatch blew open early
On the space capsule that sank
Before it could be ferried
To the USS *Something*.

The astronaut who swam out
Was a stranger. So odd, each time,
His filmed smile and greeting, he seemed
Invaded by aliens,
His cells breeding a green race.
He'd been trying to die, knew

What he'd carried back from space,
But there was rescue, the navy
Saving him for further study.

Listen, no matter how often
Someone punched out forever,
A fresh hire hurried past him
Immediately, allowing
The soul of slavery to flee
One body for the steady,
Working safety of another.

PLAYING SLEEPLESS

To slowly kill their prisoners, the ancient
Romans invented "the waking torture"—
Sleep a little. Rise. Sleep a little. Rise.

So once a day, during hell week, pledges
Flopped to the floor for twenty-minute naps,
Shaken and screamed back to the awful light

Of loyalty and brotherhood and all
The fraternity somethings to believe.
Rousted from such slumber, we understood

One thing about death, voices above us,
Hands slapping our faces while down the hall
Someone showered, someone woke to the time

And weather on the radio, choosing
Which shirt to wear, whether to dress at all
As we were taken to push-ups, mile runs,

And footballs slammed into our freshman guts
While I swore to myself my pledge brothers
Would quit before me, that I could live through

Anything by not being the weakest
Whose ribs cracked, who blacked out, who vomited
Back the soap-laced beer, the forced Vaseline

As if collapse were unacceptable
Confession, giving up the private code
For what's endurable, even if it
Hides nothing but the record for lost sleep.

THE MAN WHO NEVER SLEPT

In the library, under
The record for no sleep,
Are twelve days verified
And a paragraph about
The man who never slept.

In Trenton, New Jersey, where
Al Herpin stayed awake, teams
Of watchers tested him:
For months. At random. Like
Urinalysis for slumber.

To keep alert, those referees
Rotated. Their open eyes
Proved Al Herpin was straight,
And, it turned out, healthy,
Staying awake to 90.

You could say Al Herpin was
The world's oldest man, that he
Lived to 120
If you adjusted for
The inflation of wakefulness.

Look, a man slept forty hours
After ten days' insomnia,
So who, extrapolating
On the graph for sleeplessness

Would fault Al Herpin's fear of rest?
After a while, he had years
Of sleep stored deep. Nodding off
Meant the mind unraveling
So far and so long it could
Never be rewound. Like losing

Abstractions. Like forgetting
Names and dates that approach
From behind until the past is
A synaptic slur of blots.
Like Al Herpin demonstrating

There are maps for myth born
Into all of us. When we
Decipher the private code
Of scale, our journeys might have
A sleepless surge of distance.

THE BILLION HEARTBEATS OF THE MAMMAL

"Feel this," my father says, guiding my hand
To the simple Braille of his pacemaker.
"Sixty," he tells me, "over and over
Like a clock," and I mention the billion
Heartbeats of the mammal, how the life span
Can be rough-guessed by the 800 beats
Per minute of the shrew, the 200
Of the house cat, speeding through their billion
In three years, in twelve. How slowly we act,
According to our pets. How we are stone
To the frantic insects. "Not slow enough,"
He answers, summing up the math, citing
His two billion heartbeats of punched-in work,
The one billion my mother beat to do
The daily double-shift of housekeeper
And clerk until her heart softened to mush.
He's busy, now, with wiping down his floors
The way he swirled a mop through locker rooms

Before striding the push broom up and down
The grain of gym sweep, repeating the moves
Of twenty kinds of cleaning between ten
And six-thirty in the high school I used
Between eight and three-fifteen. He might have
Been following the Peterson Method
For care, learning the neat lines and ovals
Of my mother, who wrote to me, the day
She died, a perfectly scripted letter,
Pages of open vowels so nothing
She said could be misread. And even now,
In the attic, inside her black notebooks
Stacked and banded, her carefully copied
Familiar quotes, the good advice
Of the writing exercise dating back
To a hundred lines of ovals, fifty
Of the properly slanted line. Penciled
Pages of strict, block printing, the two-space
Capitals, the touch of tall letters to
The roof of lines, my father repeating
The multiplication and division
To the thirty years of humans, how he is
Closing in on three billion while I am
Nearing two. How we are the exception
To the heartbeat system, taking so long
To come of age we have time to practice
The Peterson Method for memory,
Preserve these things to open up and read.

THE ANCIENT CURES

My sister who cannot sleep
turns to herbs and crystals, beads
arranged in an order set
centuries ago by God.
She explains the old secrets
of chanting just so, shows me
a dark fork tuned exactly
to the pitch of the perfect

substitute for counted sheep,
forcing me to think *silly,*
then *crazy,* then whatever
a good night's sleep cannot cure.
Harmonies. Auras. Lather
from blue soap prepared with prayer.
She buys from a catalogue
for anti-despair, candles
and statues of naked gnomes.
And when, upstairs, I lower
my hand to a sprite's green head,
pressing down my palm as if
combing neat a cowlick, she
whispers "Yes" and squeezes shut
her eyes, keeps them closed until
I am a medium for rest.

THE NUMBERED DAYS

There are flowers that flourish
Through each stage of the sun, taking
Their names from time: Four o'clocks,

Morning glories, the day-long
Staying power of sunflowers.
And there are flowers, arranged,

That mark the hours of daylight,
Opening at twelve o'clock
Like passion flower, closing

Mid-afternoon, like hawkbit
And bindweed, three and four P.M.
Like white water-lily shutting

In on itself at five, evening
Primrose miraculously
Opening at twilight six

As if taking on the night shift
Of nature, punching in for
The difficult work of beauty.
"So teach us to number our days,"
The Psalmist says, and we do
Or go to the madness of waste.

So we use any hour for work,
Surrender, at last, to sleep and
Splash down to opportunity

After great arcs of renewal,
Remembering like clocks that
Know they will fail, finally,

To remember, mastering
The lesson of our numbers,
And working to make them matter.

2

Marking the Body

My doctor, a woman, knows how shyness
Shrinks men gone vulnerable in the groin.
She waits while they unbutton or unzip,
Turns from me this morning, giving me time
To excuse myself with a just-learned story:

Behind a curtain, once, women would mark
A female doll exactly where they hurt:
Just below the breasts, for instance, covered
By the doll's uplifted arm, they charcoaled
A cross; low in the belly they scratched an X.

My doctor knows that history; she says
My male doll has Xs over the lungs,
Cross-hatches on the throat, skipping the spot
For this morning's mark, the way I've never
Been this slow to undress for her instruments.

My doctor, who knows when eternity
Begins to form far out in the future's
Ocean, covers her hands in the latex
Of discretion, reaches for me, and says,
"The feet of those draperied women were bound."

My doctor, who would have passed that Barbie
To the discreet hands of a physician,
Examines me like a familiar doll.
She breathes high on my naked thighs, that air
The first that fails to stir the stiffening blood.

She pivots, strips her gloves, and I follow
The intimate lines of her breasts and hips
To the softness of myself, fixed until
She turns, finally, in the last moment
When we both are deciding what's arriving.

The Vanishing of Forlorn Hope

After the suicide mission, after
Almost all the crazy convicts are killed,
One of the living hollers, "We made it,"
And before you can say "Shut up," he's shot,
Celebrating, too soon, impossible
Survival. An old, old story, that one,
For in the beginning, just soldiers had
Forlorn hope, especially the luckless
Selected to be first up the ladders,
First from the trenches, first to march, in rank,
Across uphill, half-miles of open fields,
Dying for that phrase so often no one
Heard it change to *God's will be done,* looking
Across the river to where the drowned child
Might pull himself up the opposite bank.
What I heard was *A snowball's chance in hell,*
What I had of getting rich and famous.
According to my teachers, who, at last,
Repeated *fat chance* like a chronic cough.
Entering the Heinz plant five days a week,
I gave myself *no chance* of returning,
And then did. Mopping floors, I said *No way,*
And then punched in to soaped sponge and buffer,
Cleaning up the classrooms where those teachers
Could have found me between midnight and six.
In the evolution of expressions,
The fittest survive, though I wasted years
Until I said *No,* eliminating,
Finally, every unessential word,
Blurting refusal's unqualified hope,
Spontaneous and straightforward and heard.

The Extension of the Dead

Getting drunk, a friend called women
He had slept with, men he hated,
And then 911, repeating
"Emergency" like a schoolboy.

"Try 999," I suggested,
Giving him the hot-line number
That Malaysians, once, imagined
Was the extension of the dead,

Their calls, instead, directed to
The homes for police and firemen
And medical help, dispatchers
Picking up for thousands who thought,

Immediately, they had linked
With the calm voices of the dead.
Cautions? Disclaimers? Those callers,
Regardless, asked about heaven's

Lifestyle, what it meant to be dead.
They chanted incantations to
Ward off whatever might travel
Through phone lines from the afterlife.

"What's the story with you," my friend
Kept on repeating, receiving
Sympathy, curses, threats, a fine.
And the Malaysians? They, at last,

Asked for help with the lottery—
Because surely the selfless dead
Knew the winning numbers, the sort
Of thing you heard in paradise.

The Celestial Bed

Tonight, I'm listing the therapies
I could pay for: water and needles,
Electricity, machine-made sounds
Slithering past shrill to silence or
Deepening to inaudible bass.

I'm remembering an early one,
James Graham's Celestial Bed, how
He profited from sex therapy,
Couples lying together for light
And music and movement so subtle
They believed the ceiling's fixed star-field
Was spinning overhead like heaven.

Sometimes, there are deceits so disguised
By desire they're redesigned like myths:
In two hundred years a magician
Would make the Statue of Liberty
Disappear, the audience platform
Turning so slowly the witnesses
Surrendered to wonder's fogged pleasure.

And even now, I can concentrate
On the therapy of photos spun
Into nostalgia's constellations:
A child smiling, the light on hoarfrost,
The shadowed foundation of a home.

Though when Graham's patients, at last, stood up,
Their cures turned as vacant as magic.
The sullen fundamentalism
Of devotion made them stare and stare
Until the darkness among the stars
Showed the sky was wrong with emptiness,
Their first steps a stagger back to need.

So Use It

So much more than terror she suffered,
The woman who was certain she'd been shot.
To hold her brains inside, she pressed both hands
To the back of her head, bringing, at last,
Paramedics to the mall, men who saw
Canned bread dough had exploded inside
The oven of her heat wave car, flattening
Against her head like hysteria's spitball.
Carried off in cars, that woman's story
Was passed around dinner tables like salt,
One witness, finally, saying, "She could
Have saved Kennedy she pressed so hard."

How we interpret what we hear and feel:
The face of Jesus seen on burritos
Stacked upon a counter, the troll of death
Burned into the crust of seeded rye.
For seven years I handled bread dough
In the bakery before my father
Sized it into full loaves and sandwich buns.
More than once, after three A.M., he said,
"You have a brain, so use it," intending
My anger to put that dough behind me.

So I remember enough, now, to think
That pie-filling would be more apt for brains,
The sweet ooze of crushed berries and corn starch
Swelling up through fingers, no matter
How heavily we press, until we know,
Suddenly, we're still thinking, wondering
What part of who we are is seeping down
Our hands and over our wrists to confuse
Our fear, running up our arms like long-term
Memory, leaving us in the present.

And the woman who thought her dough was brains?
There's no denying how lucky she felt
Skipping past embarrassment to the great
Relief of recovery. Though what did
She think, driving off, of the silly name
She'd given herself with public panic?
That her story would be spread like a case
Bound over for court? That she was never
Alive until she bungled the exam
Of common sense, holding her head as if
She wasn't already as good as dead?

The Resurrection Manual

At Gettysburg, touring, I meet
A businessman struck by lightning
Who says, leaving the Peach Orchard,
He occasionally forgets
Where his next sentence is heading,
His speech creeping down a crosshatched,
Country road, even the cautious
Cursing when he parks just two wheels
On the soft shoulder of thought to
Recall which turn he intended,
And I tell him my neighbor limps,
Revived after thirty-seven
Minutes under winter water,
How she slurs short sentences like
A drunken schoolgirl, forgetting
The algebra of attachments.

More of us than you think, he says,
Sixteen over there, gesturing
Toward Little Round Top where pictures
Are being snapped by survivors,
He explains, of heaven's spiked fire,
Each of them supposed to be dead.
More of us than you think, he says,
Struck and saved, have you read this book
I have here, *The Uncertainty*
Of the Signs of Death? and he raps
On its cover as if to sound
"I'm here," telling me it's the Bible
For finding the Lazarus way.

All these stories are true, he says,
Citing the Swedish gardener
Trapped under pond ice for hours,
The German woman three full days
Under water, and the Swiss boy,

Record-holder, who was revived
After seven weeks of drowning,
A United Nations of hope.
Believe it, he says, their great gasps
Of resurfacing, and I nod,
Letting him instruct me with myth,
Remedies, finally, for those
Merely dead in their beds, listing
Onions and horseradish under
The nostrils, garlic on the gums,
And hideous shrieks in the ear
Of choice. All else failing, he says,
Pour hot wax on the forehead, press
A razor where harm won't follow.

And when the survivors begin
To retrace Cemetery Ridge,
When they wave and aim cameras
At this field, I stride beside him,
Matching steps as if we were in
Rehearsal for re-enactment.
What did those gray-clad soldiers think?
That the charge was a thunderstorm,
That, if struck, they might be revived
By readers of the *Signs of Death*?
And if we two were fatally
Stricken on this clear afternoon,
Somebody would open the book
Beside us, and learning quickly,
Surely slice the soles of our feet?

The Basic Defense of Simple Things

Once, thousands of worms were trained by science,
Shocked just after brilliant light. They wised up,
Those planaria; they cringed when their world
Went repeatedly white; but my father,
After bypass, returns again to fat.
He explains the mechanics of splitting
Spare ribs, and the words for this argument
Form from failure into a flock's sharp squawks.
There were birds, years back, that learned to open
Milk bottles, tugging off the cardboard tabs
On lids, poking holes in the foil caps
To get at cream. Lactose intolerant,
Those birds hated the homogenized age,
Flew elsewhere in the era of skim milk.
So few deliveries now, yet they look
For the cap color that says unstirred, swoop
To the last of the doorstep milk, timing
Their dives for the rare pleasure of richness.

What we remember: My father's flying
Back to marbled meat; my mother settling
Over and over on salt while I peck
At the sealed lids on anger and regret.
This can't work, we mutter, like those who scoffed
At the scientist who claimed, finally,
The memories of his worms could be learned
By larger worms who ate them, those feeders
Curling more quickly, when light exploded,
In the basic defense of simple things.

3

The Busy Darkness

WHAT THE OPTOMETRIST SAID

The eyes facing forward means predator,
Along the sides of the head declares prey.
Better here? Worse? Any difference at all?
To find our way in darkness, we must have
Six times more light than panthers. To make out
Danger, we need ten times more light than toads.
Try these. They'll fit a face as thin as yours.

The rhinoceros sees so terribly
It charges large rocks, occasional trees.
You can stop squinting now. It's a habit
You've formed through neglect. Don't you see yourself?
What do you think? Your eyes aren't corrected?
That there's too little light? That you can't see
What's approaching before it gets too close?

WRITING LETTERS FOR THE BLIND

For fifteen cents, or twenty, in the script
I'd mastered from Miss Hartung, I wrote
Saturday letters for Bill Nelson, who
Sat blind with a white cane beside his chair.
He loved the letters in return, the lines
Scratched out in pencil or blue ball-point ink.
This is Gary writing, he had me say,
And women, often, when they wrote, added
Postscripts that began *for your eyes only*
As if I wouldn't read their words aloud.
Such a dear, they repeated. *God bless you.*
We should all have such a generous son.
When one woman had her daughter write me,
She folded that page inside her letter
So Bill Nelson, holding the envelope,

Smiled and said, "It's a good one, two pages."
Straight out, that girl said her mother wanted
Us to meet, that the slope of my letters
And my way of crossing ts showed I was
A boy to be trusted when we were grown.

Before he paid me in nickels and dimes
From a change purse open on the table,
Bill Nelson measured every coin by touch.
A test, for sure, because everybody
Knew the blind heard better than the sighted,
And I passed for months, not stealing, until
A woman mailed a dollar postscripted
For me. It lay so quietly, so thin
On the table I read, "The five dollars
Are for Gary," giving myself a raise.
Would Bill Nelson believe I was worth it?
Would he consider his coins and add them
Higher in my hand? In fact, I hoped so,
Because I wouldn't steal, taking nothing
From the blind but what I thought I deserved.

THE ERA OF THE VARI-VUE

"He can see shadows," my father told me,
"Bright light and pitch dark," as if Bill Nelson
Had time-traveled from the Bible's first day.
From a front seat, squinting, I could copy
My teacher's chalked words; from my desk I could
Recognize friends' faces four rows away.
The spring I was failing that blackboard test
And the exam of the curveball, I thought
Everybody saw with the soft focus
Of myopia, hunched down to pages.

In the first, fad years of the Vari-Vue,
My father brought home plastic-ribbed pictures
Of Plymouth Landing and Christ on the Cross.
The proper distance, he said, the right tilt

Of the head until I wig-wagged Pilgrims
Ashore; the eyes of Jesus to heaven;
And signed, bobbing my head, a small, slightly
Blurred, Declaration of Independence.

Dog-at-the-hydrant. Cow-over-the-moon.
Finally, I wore glasses. By the time
I mastered contact lenses, I could shift
Nixon's eyes in the White House windows, could
Surface my children's skulls and nod my wife
To bones, flicking her forward, fast or slow,
Like mutoscope women you could undress,
Once, for a nickel.
                                        Now, for quarters, men
Can lock up in booths to watch looped films, choose
Sound-suffused channels on the porn network,
Sighed syllables of acquiescence flung
Like dots on this page I'm holding tonight,
In the gallery of unimportance,
Trusting they will leap up as holograms.

I'm staring at a near-wash of purple,
Coaxing "halved spheres" or "peeled fruit" off paper.
I'm deciphering instructions, learning
The sure ways to 3-D without glasses,
Pulling the page haze-close, one simple step
To "deep sight," the trompe l'oeil of computers
If we posture ourselves like the near-blind.

You enter the page, the inventor claims,
And I imagine the third dimension
Of pornography, toxins surfacing
In lakes, futures embossed by tainted blood.
I call each of my chattering, clear-lensed
Children to these pictures, say "hold this close
And stare," prodding them to levitate balls
And fruit, say "pear" and "globe" as if these were
Rorschach blots for the willingness to see.

REMEDIES

The Sioux believed in opening the eyes
To the dust of bezoar stones they found
In the bodies of buffalo and deer.

The British, once, believed in the power
Of baking a black cat's head to powder
For blowing in the eyes three times a day.

And some of the nearsighted, more squeamish,
Have worn gold earrings, trusting the bright loops
To recall the radiance of vision.

PUSHING THE BLACK THREAD

Hagop Sandaldjian, the world's only microminiature sculptor, was described as "a very calm man."

Last night I couldn't thread a needle.
I took it under three kinds of light;
I licked that thread; I ran it between
My fingers and thought luck, finally,
Would pull it through while I remembered
The man who sculpted between heartbeats,
How he kept his hand steady enough
To carve Snow White and the Seven Dwarves,
Red Riding Hood, and Cinderella,
Each sculpture so tiny he placed them
In the slim eyes of sewing needles.

What he carved can't be seen unaided.
For all I knew, his lost Mickey Mouse
Deflected my thread that threatened art.
"May all your dreams come true," that sculptor
Etched along one hair, but he used lint
For Presidents, dust motes for the Pope,
And I pressed my chest, at last, against
A high-backed chair, studied my pulse for

The instant of greatest calm, pushing
The black thread, failing, pushing again,
Listening and listening with light.

NOT THE WORST

Not the worst, the doctor says, matching
Me to his patient list. Not the worst,
Sounding so rehearsed I imagine
The patient who only sees shadows,
Welcoming, whore-like, whatever moves.

In the country of perfect vision,
Would anyone record what was seen?
And gone into exile, would those eyes
Wear themselves dry with excessive use?

Look. Gaze. Watch. Stare. When every edge turns
To haze, when persistent fog compares
Our hope to the hell of indistinct,
We listen for the breath of beauty,
The custodian of clarity,
Sweeping, unable to keep us clean.

BETTER, BETTER, WORSE, BETTER

Last night I woke and saw nothing and knew
It was my Bill Nelson dream, the one where
He makes change in the dark, handling each coin
In his black purse until he's satisfied
Which ones are proper. I imagine him
Cheating himself; I imagine keeping
His quarters and lying about the blind,
How they mistake coins the way I misread,
With my fractioned vision, the brief rebus
Of road signs, the puzzle of passersby.

This evening, I trust my sight to the eyes

Of my neighbor, the optometrist, who
Listens as I say *"Our Hearts Keep Singing,"*
Describing the album by the Braillettes,
Three blind women beaming good attitude
And bright hope from their cover photograph.
"It's on *Heart Warming Records,*" I finish,
Taking air puffs between blinks to confirm
It's not glaucoma that's sucking my sight.

I stammer, "Better, better, worse, better."
I hear diopters, thickness, the great curve
Of this year's inadequate correction.
The doctor hums the ceiling tunes. Follow
The light, he croons. Now ignore it. Although
I want to say "How?" half-expecting him
To switch it off, smiling in the darkness
At optometrist humor. "Worry you?"
He'd say. "Got you to thinking?" plummeting
The room to black, waiting for my answers,
My optimistic eyes still dilating,
Whether or not I'll be sadly clever
With compensatory, heartfelt singing.

HOW THE OPTOMETRIST ENCOURAGED CALM

During panic, when your mouth dries,
Breathe out until the count of six.
Breathe in until four. Count slowly.
One, two, three . . . more slowly than that.

Try to remember it's just your brain
Mimicking the symptoms you dread:
Breathlessness. Dizziness. The chest
Going tight, tingling through the hands.

Better yet, recognize your fear
Is only anticipation.
Fight it with facts. Be specific.
Darkness is danger not yet here.

4

The Sin Diseases

From the corrupted humors of the sufferers
Lice were born, rising to the surface in tumors
Of insects. And so the flesh was eaten, that death
Reserved for tyrants like Herod the Great, and those,
Like Judas, who challenged God with cheap betrayal.

Sundays, we learned which diseases were caused by sin—
Syphilis, gonorrhea, unplanned pregnancies
Swelling the bellies of our unmarried classmates.
We marveled at the sins so terrible a drop
Of them would announce your acts as it destroyed you.

Galen, Pliny, Aristotle—who would deny
The authority of the wise? Since lice could rise
From suspect blood, who might be eaten from within?
Plato, for one. And Socrates for another.
Be careful which men of science are enemies.

This morning I'm listening to my thickened lungs
Whistle that old diagnosis of damnation.
According to a friend, all the words I've written
Mean something else. When I wake up wheezing I quote
Myself and hear the thin, high breath of disbelief.

It's the failed extrapolation of the senses
That fathers faithlessness: Chatter inside a closed,
Empty room. Shoeprints in snow that suddenly stop.
We pick at our welts and boils, blisters, pimples;
Our familiar moles turn terrifyingly dark.

Running Through Directions

We drive west through Snyder County,
Back roads where the worst students live.
There, my wife says, recognizing
Names on mailboxes. There and there—
Louts and loudmouths, dreamers and dolts,
Until she murmurs "Robin Snow"
For the block-raised trailer set back
On the reclaimed township landfill,
Nothing that gives up a name but
The box number from a class card.
"Raped by the father," says my wife.
"Fourteen now, offered by the hour
To his friends." She memorizes
Details while I watch for the man
Who lives there, out, at once, on bail.
I think we aren't the first to stop,
That by now he grips a rifle
By the tiny front window where
He studies the shitheads who see
The world like tourists, suicide
Watchers, the stalkers of rubble
By fire or tornado, except
Robin Snow took tests from my wife
And carried her report cards home
To that father who attended
Open house, sitting in her desk
Among the visiting parents.
A jug-band breath of wind begins
To hum at my cracked side window;
A Plymouth veers and parks so close,
Nose to nose, we seem to tremble
In turbulence, but when I shift
To reverse, thinking it might be
The last stupid thing I will do
With my life, my wife whispers "no"
While a man steps out of that car,

Checks his watch and shades his eyes
To stare toward that trailer as if
Running through directions, matching
The box number to word-of-mouth
Advertising, not the paper
He didn't read, the radio
Turned off all morning because
He wanted to concentrate on
Where he was driving, what time he'd
Agreed, nights ago, to arrive

The Dog Shot: November 1951

The day I took home my first report card
From Wilson Street Elementary School,
A dozen sling-bound dogs were hanging
Upside down in Nevada, dressed, that day,
In cotton, orlon, or any of
The materials my parents might wear
To work or church the day the Soviets
Scattered their brand-new atomic bombs.

Those dogs, a thousand feet apart, yammered
And yapped until they were sent swinging
By a test blast. Myself, I carried home
A set of straight As in reading, spelling,
And arithmetic, excellent in
Everything, according to Mrs. Spring,
Superior on the standardized tests
We took to measure our chances in school.

Mostly, those dogs were dead, torn and roasted,
Except numbers five and nine, found alive,
Beating the radius odds to survive.
In our three upstairs rooms, the headline
Was my perfect scores, the newspaper left
For people who had time and money;
A television impossible
As a dog forbidden by a landlord.

One of those dead test dogs was warmer
Than the others, meaning he outlasted,
The scientists said, the shock and heat,
Something positive among those wounds.
My mother propped my card on the table
While we ate macaroni and cheese.
All this, she told me, will happen again
In January, in April, in June.

The Plagues in Order

For Children's Day, for the church pageant
Performed by the primary classes
Taught by the Misses Shuker and Swope,
We were the plagues in order, changing
Costumes while Moses spoke, returning
Ten times to taunt the unbelievers.

In crimson sheathes, we were the river
Turned blood. Masked and hopping, we were frogs.
And when we heard, crawling and flapping
As lice and flies, the *ohs* of adults
From the pews of Etna's Lutheran Church,
We knew a day's praise was seething for
The holy revenge of our costumes.

Like cattle, then, we went to all fours,
Lowing and listening to Miss Swope,
Who spoke for God from the balcony,
Promising the plagues to everyone
Who hardened his heart like a Pharaoh.
Like Egyptian cattle, we buckled
And fell to the side-sprawl of dying.

Look, there was more. We all wore white hoods
Circled by the red of boils, flung
Brown rice as hail before we chattered
Like locusts and swarmed off to black-sheet
Our bodies, waiting for Miss Shuker
To switch the church to darkness we made
Darker, shivering like just-freed souls.

And when we caught the collective hush,
The first-born among us dropped and died,
The rest solemn despite being blessed
By the lottery of birth, standing

To the sides like two halves of a sea,
Walking in wide pairs from front to back
To the street as if we expected
Our chastened families to follow.

The Leukemia Student

While my father and his brothers argue
The A bomb to Moscow, their wives hush them
With pig's feet and liverwurst, olive loaf
And summer sausage, three-bean salad,
Pickled eggs and my mother's brief prayer
That blesses our food and the wisdom
Of God "that passes all understanding."

And as we eat, one aunt insists the crow
That lit on her clothes post stared sickness
Through her son's west window, that she knows
The same one returned, this week, with death.
She passes the oil of sardines, blind
Robins salted by the wisdom of God.
And later, when my father scatters

Twenty of his records on the carpet,
The crow's luck past all understanding,
I become the four year old who can
Choose the requested 78s,
Not reading, because I've fixed the color
Of labels to the shape of titles,
Selecting, by memory, the tunes

His brothers want to hear, handing up
The next one, then the next, as perfect
As the wisdom of God, passing all
Understanding and receiving praise
In one of the three upstairs rooms we rent
In Etna, in 1950, after
My cousin, twice my age, has been buried

With books in each hand for his lessons,
Taking homework to heaven, according
To his mother, who claps when I finish,

As if I am brilliant, able, if asked,
To certify the wisdom of God,
What passes all understanding, by
Sorting an eternity of records.

Never Again

THE YEAR BEFORE MY LAST CHILD WAS BORN

When I slapped my son in the butcher shop,
When he whined or wiggled or reached to touch
The warned against, the butcher trimmed and trimmed
Until the porterhouse was lean enough
For a wounded heart. He slid wax paper
On the scale, read the result for so long
He might have mislaid the mathematics
Of selling. My son said nothing. I paid.
But outside my wife said "never again,"
Repeated it once, then pivoted, and
Aimed herself ahead of us like a guide.

HAD NOT

Had she not been sick, the evening
she believed me dead, my mother
would have followed the bloodhounds.
Had she not been bedridden
by high fever, she would have walked
the banned route of the railroad tracks.
Had my aunt not been nursing her
upstairs, where we rented three rooms,
she would have risen, regardless,
to sit sentry for the first news
of the police chief's posture.
Had not the man who sold sodas
refused me ice water, shouting,
after three days of saying *Yes,*
I wouldn't have walked to A&P
to drink from its ice-cold fountain.
Had not the creek and tracks been
across the street, I wouldn't have

followed them past the mill and picked
my way to the Allegheny.
Had not a man, in Pittsburgh, killed
a child the week before. Had not
boys drowned or fallen under trains.
Had not I been five years old
and wanting to fight in Korea
like our neighbor missing in action.
Had not my mother read me
Little Orphan Annie so I thought
being lost would make me rich.
Had not a man asked me where I lived.
Had not he said polio and
typhoid as if they were swimming
with the carp. Had not he walked me
through Sharpsburg so much a father
the two of us passed a policeman
who was looking for the dead.
Had not he held my hand until
Grant Avenue sloped upward to
Angle Alley and the rooms upstairs
where my mother listened for the door
because she believed me dead.
Had not I needed to unlock it
because we didn't have anything
like the A&P's electric eye.
Had not we owned a bell which rang
as I passed through like a customer.
Had not my aunt raised her hand
to me and cursed that stranger,
my mother would not have swayed
at the top of the stairs, saying "No,"
as if I were home to choose candy
or ice cream for dinner, as if I
expected her to smile and offer
cold water with my chocolate.

SMART BOY

Such a smart boy, that May, I unlocked
The back door each weekday and walked
Away from punishment for bringing

Terror to our three upstairs rooms.
My mother worked while my father slept
Off his night shift, but I wanted

To bounce a ball off the warehouse,
Calling myself Bullet Bill Dudley
And Billy Conn because I'd heard

Those names blessed by my father. I knew
A hundred Bible verses, did
Requests for my relatives who clapped

Before they began Canasta
At card tables cornered by peanuts
And bridge mix, ginger ale and cubes

Of orange cheese. In June, the back streets
Filled up with boys who swore and threw
My rubber ball into the storm drain.

Slide down, they said, and fish for it,
And I answered, "You owe me," citing
The seven cents I'd saved and paid.

They laughed when Vern Hutka slammed his fist
Into my stomach and turned air
Into water. "How's that feel, smart boy?"

He said, but I was staring through
The bricks of Angle Alley, looking
For my ball until they were bored.

A block away, a train blew coal soot
Skyward. Across the tracks, men smoked
Outside the mill. I named the nine weeds

That were fighting up from between
The bricks. I started memorizing
For the test on the worthwhile things.

BELTS

When we visited, when dinner ended
And my cousins were supposed to behave
Like their father, sitting up straight to wait
Their turn to talk, the kitchen was a church.
I never said a word through that summer
My uncle smoked and swore and swung, just twice,
The leather belt uncoiled thick and black
From his green work pants, but my cousins' chairs
Came unbalanced, rocked and tipped to silence
Across the dark-scuffed, linoleum floor.
My uncle, a year later, lost his voice
To cancer, but those nights, before we left,
I was terrorized by the strop he used
On his straight razor. Black and wide, it hung
By the sink, nothing my father needed
For his safety razor stored like a toy.
I counted, once, in his closet, five belts,
All of them brown or black, skinny and cracked
Where the buckle-tongues tore through the third hole
As if my father never changed. I slapped,
In my room, the one belt I owned against
My flimsy arm. I whipped my bony legs.
Not one of those lashes was hard enough
To change me, sissy in a house of belts
Sheathed in slack parabolas, waiting for
My father, finally, to slap my face
For bitching about nothing, set my lips
Into dissatisfaction's welcome sneer.

SHAKING OUT THE MADNESS

"A good shaking is what you need, "Miss Hartung said,

Before she mixed and stirred us to settle things down.
The shoulder grab. The arm squeeze. She had a hand-hold
For each of our mistakes. Outside, during recess,
We claimed we could shake the shit out of each other,
Throwing the weakest down because they needed it.

Because we wanted to, we sat on swings, twisting
Their steel chains around and around and tight until
Somebody shoved, and we screamed and thrashed like crazy.
Miss Hartung watched. She showed us, one day, her pictures
Of the asylum seats a doctor built to shake
Some sense into lunatics. Not so long ago,

She told us, those chairs hung from hospital ceilings.
They shook out the madness, spun the insane for hours
To lessen the blood to the brain. Benjamin Rush,
She told us. Look him up for homework; learn what else
He did besides help the helpless. There's his statue
In the city. Go look. You'll see. You're being saved.

Smart-alec, she said, know-it-all, standing so close
We couldn't see past her face when she lifted us
From our hard-backed seats screwed into the floor. Good sense
Would come to the shaken. We could be cured in spite
Of ourselves, she would see to that, because she knew
What was right for us, just what the doctor ordered.

THE HEARSAY OF X RAYS

To calm me, the doctor
Who ordered my CAT scan
Described one-of-a-kinds
From the emergency room,
Finishing with the man
Who needed to see his brain:
"He had drilled three inches
Through his skull, and jammed,
When he saw nothing,
A coat hanger down that route

To rouse response. After that,
He was willing, thanks, to believe
The hearsay of X rays."
An inch from necessity, his hand
Brushed my hair, and I told him
My uncle with a plate in his head
Had fallen twice from a moving truck,
Before and after, telling us,
During dinner, how the asphalt sang
The shriek of short strings, how
The second truck had rolled,
Its headlights strobing the stars.
And I had said nothing, waiting for
The common pitch of disbelief
To reach my grandmother, that plate
Surely as phony as the silliness
Of Radithor she'd recalled,
Minutes before, men drinking
A radium potion and assuredly
Glowing from the aphrodisiac
Of atomic weight. "Until
They collapsed inside," she'd said,
"Never again for that, the fools,"
Pulling back, minutes later,
My arms from her shattered window,
Stemming the blood which pumped
From both wrists, saying "never again"
Like a lesson to be memorized,
Something so important I chanted
That phrase like the chorus of a song.

THE HISTORY OF POPULAR DANCES

The teacher across the hall said
She only snapped once, beating a boy
Who was doing the Mashed Potato
Beside her desk. Such a small thing,
She said, and then I was cuffing
The James Brown out of him.

She said the matter was dropped, how things
Ended in nineteen sixty-three
When lapses were human, not taken
To court like odd looks and failing grades,
And I recited the three times I'd been
Whacked that year, including the textbook
Head slap, the knee raised from behind.

For doing the Limbo in the hall,
One boy was thumped, a teacher fed up
With the evils of Chubby Checker.
Those parents, I said, won apology,
And I recounted the silence
And the broom handle swept upright
Like the boy I'd just slammed against
The cinderblock of my classroom.

You tell them and you tell them,
That woman said, and then one teacher
Told us he challenged, fists formed,
Every boy in his classes. The first day
Of school, twenty years now, and then
Nobody dances or says a word,
And I nodded because the boy
Who had shouted at me had shut up
And sat down like everybody else
In that classroom so I could talk
About grammar or poems or
The history of popular dances,
Ending with the Popcorn, one they'd learned
That winter, one they could climb out
Of their desks to demonstrate if I
Told them to as I began to sing.

BLUE MOON

In 1977, just after my vasectomy,
a man in Somalia contracted
the last natural case of smallpox.

Twenty years now, as long ago
as the death of Elvis, but there are
17 million vaccine doses in storage,
"Just in case," according to
the Elvis sighters of disease.
Though why not, those germs sampled
and stored as well, a neighbor,
each August playing "Blue Moon" at sunset,
spinning it 42 times to honor
the Elvis life span. I've thanked him
for not adding the posthumous years,
for not playing the all-day Elvis canon,
those songs so common I anticipate
the words. In Bangladesh, the word
for smallpox is the same as the word
for springtime, another version
of common, but I ask my neighbor
why not "Blue Moon of Kentucky" or
"When My Blue Moon Turns to Gold Again,"
and he asks, "What were you doing when
Elvis died?" and I know I was listening
to the cries of my last-born son, that
my wife was feeding him, give or take
an hour, and I was wishing him
the good luck of the gold moon because
chance had already been recorded.

THE POINTILLISM OF ABUSE

In the middle of his yearbook, my son
Has shown me a picture of the woman
Who's beaten her baby to death, who's heaved
That child against a wall and inflicted,
According to the news, a hundred wounds.

In the middle of his yearbook, she smiles
Two photos from my son, four years ago,
Senior class at the high school I've just passed,
But right now she pauses at the crosswalk,

Waits across from me for the light to change.

In the middle of his yearbook, *alleged*
Keeps its secret, *autopsy* doesn't speak,
Alibi refuses the down payment
For bail. In the middle of his yearbook,
She's not made, like now, from the billion dots

Of pointillism, spaces among them
I can see as if my vision has switched
To ten power, one hundred, whatever
It takes to make out the way we're packaged
And sent through the distance between us,

Each coroner's catalogued bruise spreading
The flat features of her face until I
Pass the luminous screen of her body,
Slip behind it like a child expecting
To see a dog just disappeared from view.

BUYING FOR THE WEEK OF CHANGE

The day after my third child
Was born, I was a father
In cereal, buying for
The week of change. My daughter
And son stopped as often as dogs.
They raised boxes like models,
Spouting sugar flakes, prizes
Packaged inside, their language
Shrill and foreign with begging.
The ceiling speakers tracked us
Like security. We'd come
From the hospital to meat
And poultry; to snack food, soda,
And those songs so steadily
Pouring the floors seemed slick
Just before the table where
A woman offered samples

Of cookies, four of them dark
On a plate like scattered thoughts.
My son took one without asking,
A second like a thief; Shannon
Scrabbled both hands so close behind
That when I hammered her twice, front
Of my hand and back, she dragged
Him down beside the blue shoes
Of the saleswoman, all of us
So suddenly silent we seemed
To be listening for the next
Recorded song, ready to scream
Its title like contestants.

NEVER AGAIN

How frail our claims to be anything, that
We're measured by pain endured like
St. Appolonia, whose teeth were pulled
For not renouncing an indifferent God,
Another operation performed
With the anesthesia of "never again,"
Each repetition the first reply
From paradise. As if it could voodoo
Somebody like the man, this week,
Who tied a child to a tree and raped her.
Because, he said, he wanted to be
Executed, he chose a crime to earn it.
I've passed that tree with my daughter,
Handled its leaves without anticipating
The apocalypse of failure, the chorus
Of "never again," what this day's demon
Repeats each time a camera swings his way,
So much genesis in his squall of voice
There's no telling if someone will shoot him
A million times to test the record,
Something like the miles of Plennie Wingo,
Who hiked backwards to Turkey from southern
California so "never again" seemed true;

Like Edward Mordake, born with two faces,
Front and back, two extra eyes which cried,
An extra mouth which drooled and gibbered
Mirror language, babbling things "They only
Speak of in hell," how Mordake put it
Before killing himself, fearing that face
"Would continue its dreadful whisperings
In my grave," saying *never again,* face forward,
Repeating faith's basic phrase, listening
For the sibilant voice which might follow

5

Miss Hutchings Takes the Girls in Our Health Class Aside for the Lesson on Horned Women

First, the German nun who went mad
When the French invaded her convent.
Who banged her head, for years, against
A table, until, above one eye,
A horn emerged, curing madness
As it grew, restoring her to God.

And soon the theory of climate,
That certain countries had the weather
For horns, sheep and goats and women.
Soon after, the theory of anger,
The woman who claimed her horns grew
From quarreling with her son, such rage
At his actions she itched above
Her ear until she scratched free her spike.

But always, the devil theory,
The cases like Mrs. Burnby's, who
Married at 50, according
To her neighbors, for "impure motives,"
Breaking down after the "I dos,"
Sprouting a horn so quickly, nothing
Doctors could say or write about
Tumors or trauma could sway people
From the old religion of horns.

The devil waits just below the skin
Of our skulls, his horns commanded
To rise by flaws, an explanation
Louder than textbooks, how we
Are remembered, finally, by place,
By disposition, and by sin,
That first tiny bump examined by
Tentative fingers, the turning,

This way and that, to a mirror,
The subsequent daily inspections,
The wishful thinking, the moment
Of being first recognized by men.

The Brain Shelter

Almost always, in the saved-brain movies,
Someone smart or evil needs a body.
They have heads; we recognize their faces;
The surgeons search for the young and pretty.
But those brains without a skull, what of them?
Only when the sauce they're kept in bubbles
Do we know they're thinking hard about odds,
Angry, aroused, or in despair over
The difficulties of disembodied faith.

In England, inside an old bomb shelter,
Eight thousand brains float in formaldehyde,
And we know, touring the display so near
A psychiatric hospital, past wards
Of patients are arranged here, their brains bought
For candy or a shopping spree for toys.
Alzheimer's, we read, schizophrenia,
Parkinson's, Pick's disease, repetitive
Concussions from padded fists. Look, we hear,
This brain is shriveled, this one is compressed,
Two of the thousand shapes for the mind gone wrong.

It's enough to spark the old words for loss:
Moron, dufus, imbecile, we begin;
Idiot and loony, fuckup, goofball,
Nut case, shell shocked, or the complexity
Of gradual loss, my friend describing
The dark spots on his MRI, places
Where nothing will return to remind him
Of the small, automatic ways to move,
Where he stared and stared, expecting something
In the night sky of his brain, if only
The conditions were right as he squinted
While the doctor declared, "See? There?" as if
Those words were double entendre for repair.

Child Stars

During fifth grade, when pen pals were assigned,
Miss Logue passed out a list of ten year olds
In Canada because, she said, countries
Other than ours were there to be studied.
Paula Phelan, who wrote to movie stars,
Carried a letter just come from Cubby,
The boy on *Tales of the Foreign Legion.*
The following day, encouraged, she passed
Around one from Rusty of *Rin-Tin-Tin,*
And another from Timmie, who was saved
Each Sunday by dependable Lassie.
They didn't live in Canada, where schools
Were filled with students we never heard of.
And worse yet, the day we wrote our letters
She brought a note from Patience and Prudence,
Who sang "Tonight, You Belo-ong to Me"
And were adorable like the Lennon
Sisters, who never replied. My pen pal,
Who lived in Halifax, wrote half a page,
But I filled three sides for extra credit,
Remembered the comma after Dear Brad,
And correctly spelled out *Sincerely yours.*

I thought everybody would get an A
For friendly letters, but Ronnie Riggs wrote
Just one sentence, making his letters huge,
And Don Gebert scrawled "I hate this damn school"
On the back as if Miss Logue wouldn't check
When she inspected for errors, circling
The empty space for the return address,
The spot where Eddie Hoak forgot his stamp.

On our televisions, in black and white,
Patience and Prudence wore pointed white shoes
And dark dresses puffed out by petticoats.
Their letter to Paula Phelan was typed

And said they were happy she loved their song.
Somebody was writing them a new one.
You'll hear it soon, they promised, but no one
Ever did, that record, if they made it,
Leaving like the letter of Audrey Weeks,
Who wrote her own name and address twice
On the white envelope, getting it back
The next day as if she'd answered herself.

Distraction Therapy

To overcome fear, count backwards
(start anywhere) by threes and eights.
Or multiply—the times tables

Can soothe the heart. To slow breathing,
tap your feet. Do knee bends. If you
hum melodies, you will believe

you are dancing. To stop panic,
try anagrams or spell the names
for where you are. Find all the words

within them. Keep track of your score.
To break anxiety, focus
On something far in front of you.

Walk toward it, totaling your steps.
To manage the next bad moment,
press one hand against the other.

To manage the one after that,
grip them tight and begin to pull.
The hands are antidotes. Pit one

against the other. See? Each time
you fight yourself, you smother fear.
To keep from dying, remember

the times you've survived. That list holds
all the terrors you imagine.
Read them aloud—then breathe, then breathe.

The Piecework of Writing

Eidetic is the term for mental images so clear
and vivid they are photographically sharp.

SHORTHAND

One evening, my mother wrote everything
I said, smiling as my sentences sped
Into a stutter of stupid phrases
That spoke the idiot in me when she
Read each one exactly back from shorthand.

In her notebook was nothing but the curves
And squiggles of crib-art, and when, angry,
I speed-read each verse of the longest Psalm,
She recited from those scribbles as if
She were cued by the whispered voice of God.

WRITING EVERYTHING

In the next county, the woman
Who can't stop writing, her story
On television, followed by
The news of history's cases,
Words, then sentences, paragraphs,
Pages and pages and pages.

For privacy, she says, she built
A room. For storing her notebooks
Like William Harvey, who dug
Secret spaces under his house
In which to think, discovering,
Meanwhile, the functions of the heart
And the circulation of blood.

There, in those caves, when Harvey wrote,

He spelled pig with three gs, tripled
The last letters of *hearttt* and *blooddd,*
Shorthand for his nonstop writing,
Holding his breath with his pen hand
To hear better, perhaps, his heart.

The woman who claims she's writing
The serial book of her life
Brings a book to the camera.
Months, she says, it's taken, to work
A week into the long story
Of the difficult act of art.

"Look here," she murmurs, opening
The volume, and the reporter
Softly reads: "I began to write.
I kept writing. The light changes.
I write. I write. I write. I write,"
Sounding out a pulse, the words
Swirling, then reswirling, like blood.

THE BOOK OF NUMBERS

From one to one million, in pica type,
Marva Drew recorded all the numbers
On two thousand five hundred pages stacked
Beside her typewriter like a novel.

When I was seven, I reached ten thousand
In a weekend, filling twenty pages
Before I handed them to my mother.
"No mistakes," she said. "Good job." And I thought,

Ten thousand and one, ten thousand and two,
And went outside to bounce a rubber ball
Off the roof and a wall to simulate
Seven tense baseball games in a season

Of one hundred fifty-four, keeping track
Of runs and hits, the batting averages
Of every player, updating success
And loss, writing after every inning.

PIECEWORK

When I told the old women to slow down,
That I was tired of lugging pulled chicken
By the hundred pound, every one of them
Said "Fuck off" so fast, so uninflected,
I knew I wasn't the first food-hauler
Not to recognize the speed of piecework.
That evening I was stealing my paycheck
By the hour, as lazy as Forrest Ford
Had called us, teaching the piecework credo.
He'd meant plane geometry, the number
Of proofs we completed, the quality
Of our work. Those who counted for nothing,
The failures, Forrest Ford dared with his fists.
They needed the piecework of punishments,
Or they'd hurt somebody besides themselves.
We needed the forces of pride and shame,
Our test grades, by name, posted on his door
To say who we were in mathematics,
Where discipline was measured, teaching us,
He said, "How all are judged," nothing about
The daily tests of sexual longing,
Small expectancies for joy, those women
Hurrying steamed chicken meat to the scale,
The shadows of nearby houses running
In from the late sun that chased those women
Who scurried, by the clock, into darkness,
Their voices issuing from their thick hands
In the common language of usefulness
Mastered, as always, by the rote of touch.

THE FIVE-MINUTE DIARY OF ROBERT SHIELDS

A man, once, recorded his life in a diary divided into five minute intervals. He wrote for the piecework of words, so often and so long talking through his fingers, sleep was anxiety for the pages unwritten. He woke to the joy of "I rose and then reached for my pen." He worked the minutes into shape until twenty-four years had inched into eighty-one boxes full of five-minute diaries. When he brushed his teeth, he detailed it; while he shaved, he wrote. Everything he ate was recorded in the lines of the last few minutes.

Some mornings Robert Shields made the resolution of conclusion: *Write,* he said to himself, *This is the last line,* and then he recorded the next secrets—breakfast, the shades of light in the kitchen, how many steps he took leaving and returning to the room where the diary offered itself like pornography. Until *11:20, settling into bed, pulling up blankets.* Until *11:25, turning off the lights, writing in the dark.* Until *11:30, writing, still writing, still writing.*

MEMORIZING THE DEAD

Traveling home, after death, with snapshots,
I fail to match my memories to scenes,
Learning the limits of photography,
Nothing at all like the classmate who'd named,
After the short funeral for our friend,
Each of the forty-eight of us who'd died.

Nothing at all like Marcella Gebert,
Who ran the times tables to one hundred
One afternoon at the end of fifth grade,
Said thirty-four times seventy-six was
Two thousand, five hundred and eighty-four
Though she'd failed a grade, though she couldn't read.

Nothing at all like Cy Gillner, who sat
Up front on the bus for eleven years,
Remembering his textbooks word for word
Until the CIA hired him to crack
The Soviet Union's codes for fury.

We went to the school for coincidence,
Two savants in the neighborhood, nothing
At all like probability's classroom.
The last time I had seen my dead classmate
Was eighteen years ago at another
Reunion, but I stared at his body
This afternoon until he reappeared.

THE EIDETIC CHAMPION

Thomas Macaulay, I've read, memorized
The whole of *Paradise Lost* overnight.
So remarkable, and yet the current
Eidetic champion resides in Burma,
Reciting, so far, seventeen thousand
Pages of Buddhist books. And who proofreads
His recitation, listening for flaws?
And who wants to memorize my notebooks,
Two hundred of them to recite, twenty
Thousand pages of poetry and prose?
Who wants to read files of discarded work,
The boxes of drafts with penciled changes?
Marva Drew kept typing, hunched like a dog
That digs a hole in a front yard, beaten
And going back to start a new one, smacked
And going back again. The friend who died
Was fifty-five. After his funeral,
I drove home to four hours and twelve minutes
Of music. I heard seventy-two songs.
I sang each of them to keep from counting.

6

The Obsolescence of Surprise

Sometimes a woman knows the child she carries
Will die shortly after birth. Sometimes she picks
Taking that child to term, delaying its end.
Sometimes, too, she lives nearby, a friend who swells
And makes her neighbors consider certainty.

Sometimes, not that long ago, the pregnant feared
For the features of their about-to-be-born.
Because, too often, they'd seen spiders or snakes.
Or worse, they'd carelessly touched them, knowing change
Could enter children through the eyes and fingers.

Listen, a woman woke to find a monkey
Perched so high on her inner thigh, she gave birth,
Accordingly, to the world's tiniest child.
Sicilian Fairy, she called her daughter,
Displaying her until, nine years old, she died.

Astonishing their mothers, some infants slid
Into breathing with the facial hair of wolves
Or the snouts of pigs. In our small suburb, bare
Of animals, our neighbor, as if absence
Can harm, knows which pieces of her daughter failed.

Sometimes, screaming, a midwife would curse the quirks
Of God. Sometimes, softly, the woman we know
Names her baby's missing parts. Surprise, now, is
Obsolete. Though how we face the certainties
Of what's-to-come marks us like potent omens.

The Early History of the Submarine

In the handed-down writings of Pliny.
In Herodotus; in Aristotle.
In DaVinci, who fears The Flood's return
And sketches his own elaborate plans.
In failures. In the men who construct them
And drown. In Cornelis Drebbel, who sinks
And resurfaces, confident as God.
In his passengers. In King James the First,
Who demands a ride. In closing that hatch.
In sliding under the surface, the king
Watching the hull, listening to those walls

For the limits of greased leather and wood.
In Drebbel saying five, ten, fifteen feet.
In their settling and the king exhaling.
In the oars they pull together. In talk,
Finally, of windows and speed and air.
In Drebbel, at last, slowing his breathing
To give the king a larger share. In joy.
In surfacing with wishes he's prepared.

Otherwise Healthy

Twice this week, choosing from near the bottom
Of the list of phrases I rarely use,
I've murmured "otherwise healthy" as if
It explained the history of allergies.
The foot doctor who lives nearby has died
From a bee sting despite his antidote.
The five in my family, slouched on the deck
From summer dinner, shake our heads, listen
To my daughter tell us, a second time,
She swallowed liqueur speckled with gold dust,
And her throat shut tight as if it wanted
Nothing more. Though after she gasped and wheezed,
After her friends begged the bar for doctors,
She saw strangers stand to say "what?" and "how?"
Like magician's children, the evening's whim
Deciding, then, to soundlessly inhale.
"I could have died a metaphor," she says,
"The woman with an allergy to gold,"
And we list the odd possibilities
Of "sunshine" and "moonlight," "the songs we love,"
How we turned up our favorite music
As we walked outside on this clear day, just
Before sunset, daring the light and dark.

Birds-of-Paradise

After surgeries, after one knee
And then the other were scraped and cleaned
And made comfortable like the dying,

I swung myself on crutches, then limped,
Then slow-walked near normally until
This next breakdown of cartilage and bone.

Tonight, my father says, "Now you know,"
Phrasing satisfaction or despair
With his old rhythms for speed and bluntness.

Together, we slide and shuffle down
His stairs, do the awful one-step
To the music of irreparable.

For all it matters, for comedy,
I call out my turning radius
In a short expletive of self-pity,

Watch my father manage the minute
He needs to rise from a chair and lurch
To his collection of canes by the door.

"Some mornings," he says, "I wake thinking
My legs are amputated, yet there,
That I've been revised like your best poems,

My knees small hinges that bend just air,"
And I believe, in that moment's rhyme,
That he's prepared for me by rehearsing,

That before mobility's rapture,
We'll redesign ourselves by omission,
Taking away all the common parts

By which we are compared, becoming
Birds-of-paradise, which, because the legs
From the first specimens sent to Europe

Were removed for easier shipping,
Were thought to perpetually fly
And live by eating the dew from heaven.

How's It Going?

In the bilingual comic book,
Extending his hand and smiling,
A boy fills the overhead bubble
With "How is it going with you?"
Employing the stiffened English
Of classrooms. What do we expect
The grinning, cartoon Chinese girl
To answer? "Fine. And how are you?"
"Greetings, I am pleased to meet you"?
Not this time, her copy altered
By the stroked white of cover-up,
Fresh type that mimics the font size
And style, giving her the message:
"Fuck you, you fucking cocksuckers,"
So convincingly, one student,
I'm told, used that sentence to greet
Her new foreign-exchange family,
Shaking father's hand as she spoke.
"How's it going?" he'd said to her,
Tense as I was, blurting, first day
On the job, "How's it going, Joe,"
To the college president who
Would fire me, a few years later,
"Because, Fincke, you're not happy here."
How difficult is our learning?
I'd stuttered that phrase, at fifteen,
To Sandy Stephenson, who laughed,
Repeated it and laughed again
Outside the tenth grade home room where
I'd staked myself to ask her out.

I remember all those failures
Because that translation story
Ends with the girl's apology,
The host-mother embracing her
As if obscenity blessed them,

But this morning, coming back to
Classes, I noticed a colleague
In her darkened office, and said,
"How's it going?" before I took
Three more steps and saw the answer
In lost weight, pallor, the silk scarf
Tied tight around her skull. She forced
The brief, tentative laugh of grief,
Kept her expletives to herself,
And I thought, a moment, about
Sharing that altered scene with her,
Giving her the chance to answer
"Fuck you, you fucking cocksucker,"
Translating the cancer, holding
Out her hand or pulling it back
Because, didn't I see, she was
Hosting the foreigner, not me?

The Magpie Evening: A Prayer

When magpies die, each of the living swoops down
and pecks, one by one, in an accepted order.

He coaxed my car to start, the boy who's killed himself.
He twisted a cable, performed CPR on
The carburetor while my three children shivered
Through the unanswerable questions about stalled.
He chose shotgun, full in the face, so no one stepped
Into the cold, blowing on his hands, to fix him.
Let him rest now, the minister says. Let this be,
Repeating himself to four brothers, five sisters,
All of them my neighbors until they grew and left.
Let us pray. Let us manage what we need to say.
Let this house with its three hand-made additions be
Large enough for the one day of necessity.
Let evening empty each room to ceremony
Chosen by the remaining nine. Let the awful,
Forecasted weather hold off in East Ohio
Until each of them, oldest to youngest, has passed.
Let their thirty-seven children scatter into
The squabbling of the everyday, and let them break
This creeping chain of cars into the fanning out
Toward anger and selfishness and the need to eat
At any of the thousand tables they will pass.
Let them wait. Let them correctly choose the right turn
Or the left, this entrance ramp, that exit, the last
Confusing fork before the familiar driveway
Three hundred miles and more from these bleak thunderheads.
Let them re-gather into the chairs exactly
Matched to their numbers, blessing the bountiful or
The meager with voices that soar toward renewal.
Let them have mercy on themselves. Let my children,
Grown now, be repairing my faults with forgiveness.

www.ingramcontent.com/pod-product-compliance
Lightning Source LLC
Chambersburg PA
CBHW020809160426
43192CB00006B/495